Fractions of the Soul

Anca Milea

BookLeaf Publishing

Presentation by *BookLeaf Publishing*

Web: www.bookleafpub.com

E-mail: info@bookleafpub.com

ISBN: 9789357213127

First edition 2023

Surrender

I won't surrender my heart
Neither the earth under my feet.
I won't let my country fall apart
Neither let it burn in a pit
I won't let my voice be killed
By those who wish for fear to be built.
I will fight until my last breath
I may have my dance with death
But you won't have my country
You won't have here any victory party
You will die here and flowers will bloom
Over your dead bodies - you'll find doom
And nothing else will wait for you
'Cause we'll steal your hope too
Until you'll want to surrender
And you'll be the single bender.

Missing

I miss feeling alive
Does that make me naive?
I miss traveling until my feet hurt
And maybe just getting lost in a little flirt.
I miss getting lost in books and stories
And running in my dreams with fairies.
I miss the laughter of my friends
Before we saw our ends.
I miss how my fingers used to intertwine
With yours while calling you mine.
I miss screaming 'I love you' from the bottom of my lungs
And the feeling of happiness like I was on drugs.
I miss your green eyes and how beautiful I felt in them
And your words that made my worries scrum.
But I don't miss falling in love
Usually, for me, it never fits like a glove.
I don't miss the tears, the shouts,
The questions, the depression, not even the doubts.
I don't miss the times I surrendered my boundaries
Just to keep going those painful memories
I don't miss my voice being chocked

And my worth being locked
By somebody's else immaturity
After so much time I have clarity…
I may miss the hugs, the affection
But what's the point when there's no direction?
I may miss those old people that made me happy
But they never appreciated how I was chatty
I may miss the love of a boy
But I am no more just a toy.
So, here I am, with all these things
I miss and not, waiting for what my future
brings.

Regression

Will it ever finish with a happy ending?
Or am I in search of a desire that's too much?
Stardust in my eyes, I am losing touch
With the reality of an endless living.
I've been alive for tons of lives
That you could barely count
Others may think I try to flaunt
But my soul still rarely thrives
After countless chances to be a lifetime dealer
I am merely an endless, tired, lifeless traveller.
A peasant, a mighty empress, and a foolish healer
Name it and I probably experienced it without a cheer.
My whole existence - a compound of unfortunate events
With crime, magic, and a small tweak in historical trends.
In search of an ancient king
With dark eyes, and a desire to sing.
I search for those eyes who saw me
And didn't just look through my body
Like I was just another worthless nobody.
I am waiting for him just to be
And say my name in those starless nights

When I may be lost in pointless fights.
It would be enough to make me smile
It would be enough to make me believe
That is going to be alright after a while
If I just for once wouldn't attempt to leave.
I would fight just for him again and again
So we both know our love is not in vain
That we won't find an end
Even after we are dead.

Passion

They talk about true passion
Like it is another discussion about fashion.
I never understood how it could be so easy
To discover something for which you
Would die for - sounds so cheesy
Even more when it's just a few
That discover their calling in this life
It's almost as hard as searching for a wife.
It must be just for you, special in your eyes
Until the day you die and can't love it anymore
I wish it sounded a bit more helpful or wise
But the truth is life is just a whore to the core
It's not for those faint of heart
As it is a cheater right from your start
When it throws you on a part of the planet
Under a race, a too-toxic family, a gender
And some political pressure, all in one set.
It tries from birth to make you surrender
Under ideas and norms old as time
Nobody gives to passion a dime.
They may talk about it, even propagate
sometimes
But in the end, life is sour as a bowl of limes
It rarely gives you an untroubled life
Without the need to fight with a knife

For your deepest desires.
I swear, it burns like fires.
Thus, passion is hard to find
When you just try to survive
Society never takes into consideration
That the path to passion is full of frustration
As you first need to survive, to achieve security
Even more, to somehow work and party socially
Before you can barely think about passion
But society still lacks compassion
For those people who never find it
Hence, we just consider it
A sad and unfortunate quit.

Bad Qualities

I am a 23-years old lady, lost in London
Sounds like a cliche and full of boredom
To the surprise of my own public
I am still not hopelessly lovesick
I may love to dance and party
But I am nothing close to a Barbie.
You can get your fingers lost in my hair
And may fall enchanted by my fair skin
But my best part is how keen
I become when I want to win
I almost walk like a queen.
My arrogance is so inappropriate
After the society norms
Good thing I am not a boring portrait
As even my eyes turn into storms
Every time I become too enraged
With those norms that make me feel caged.
I could be magic as a daydream
Until I open my mouth and I scream
It's almost as an attempt to break free
From the same norms, without paying the soul fee.
The worst part is that I love to have sex
And as a lady, you lose all people respects
As only the boys should enjoy this endeavour

While for ladies is banned forever.
I could enrage my public further
As I lack the wish for kids and getting married
I prefer to be just an outsider
I wish to be neither financial carried
Because I'm a woman who runs with the wolves
So, I don't require to be treated with gloves.
Even more, as I can perfectly deal with my shit
So low standards I could never permit
As I care more about my life quality
Than about those society norms - too faulty.

Afraid

I am afraid of all I am
I am afraid of my full potential
And I shouldn't give a damn
About where it will take me
If I just don't fail…
I don't let my potential just be
Cause it will hurt
If it doesn't end up
Like a piece of art.
This cycle is a trap
For aspirations and dreams
For all the yet not existing realms
It is a trap of the soul and mind
Under a time not so kind.
I am afraid to bloom
Seems like I'll find doom
For all the words I have within
People would just throw to the bin
All my deepest fears and feelings
That I had the courage to put on a paper
With the hope that my healings
Would inspire other generations

Never ask

I didn't ask you to give up all for me
I knew myself better than to ask
You, to get on an endless quest
Without a desired happy end to be
I knew that I won't be there
To even care
For all the broken hearts
For all the stopped hertz
I knew I won't make you smile for long
We could never get our lives along
Mine is so full of unlimited experiences
Yours is static and nothing special
And for me, this will always be a crucial
Standard, I could never give up with all the aces
You may have in your pocket
Nothing will make me accept bullshit anymore
I will send all the wrong guys on a rocket
To the world of 'Never Trying Again More'.
Cause this is my biggest problem
I try too much for guys who don't give a damn
That sometimes I go up to 80s
While there is a barely return of 20s
From their so used to "have it all" ass.
So why should I care about their heart mess
When my efforts go in vain

And I am mostly in pain
For souls that never truly cared
How much I've been always scared
About what that relationship will bring next
Hence, I broke out with life through a text

You left

Was it easy to leave?
Was it easy to hear me screaming
Just because you couldn't behave?
Was it worth it? Or it had no meaning?
I had those questions in my mind
But answers were hard to find.
I still look at my pale face
You really left no trace
Of your presence in my life
Though in my heart is a knife
Deep inside it carves the word: TRAITOR
Cause my heart crowned you as its creator
And the tears fall like leaves in the autumn
But they go to the despair bottom.
And I'm left here
Hoping to be able to bear
All the people that are falsely cheering me up
The cynicism in my heart yells: it's all a trap.
But I have to smile for more than another mile
Like I should ignore the death in my heart
Although is tragic as the death on the Nile
Though I can't consider it any piece of art.

Nobody around

When nobody is going to be around
All is going to be left is you
To stand up for yourself and bound
To a new expertise that has less pain due.

When nobody is going to be around
You can finally dance in the rain
As there is no judging crowd
To force you in a further physical drain.

When everybody has left you behind
It may be easier for your smile to find
A reason to never leave from your face
As nobody will inflict pain that wants to confess
To the world how tragic life can be
You may actually have time to enjoy some tea
That's not connected to social despair or gossip
So let me give you one last tip.

After everybody left, enjoy your time alone
Feel the loneliness in a crowd, deep to the core
You may finally see how little control
Your brain thought those strangers stole
You could breathe freely in your lungs
As you did during those times when hugs

Were part of your daily life as a child.
It's time to live a bit wild
With a mind of a child in a grown-up body
It should be more than a simple hobby
To live your existence with the same curiosity
Your younger self used to love life with ferocity.

Love yourself

Love yourself when nobody else does
Love yourself on days that seem too hard
'Cause we love the flower and the spins on a rose
So why should you be so scared
Of loving yourself a bit more on gloomy days.
Stop worrying about what stranger stays
After all, when you die nobody accompanies you
So why put a wage on your happiness
When you face just a portion of the view?
Why wouldn't you watch it with some tenderness?
Nobody is more than a stranger
In your life, so stop this fear of danger.
Just breathe in, breath out
And maybe have a shot
To feel better in your skin
Maybe even have a glass of gin.

Love your wrinkles and white hair
As they witnessed your smiles and sorrows
They are a proof of all the tomorrows
That you received as an answer to your prayer.
A silent prayer that comes out with each breath

You take in and take out - a wonderful cheat of death.

Stars

Why do stars cry over the Earth?
Has it ever crossed your mind this thought?
They spend millions of years leaving in our sky
So, what makes them fall over us and die?
When did we evolve in creatures, stars need to tear for?
When did this world turned to be defined by war?
We battle with each other, we battle with ourselves
In the end, our best days become books on shelves
That we are too busy to touch.

We are the broken generation, the first to judge
Anything that even dares to move around us
Is in a second put on a blacklist with a lot of fuss.
We are the clowns the stars dare to wail
We are no prince or princess from a fairy tale
We are the dragons, the antagonists, the haters
The ones who won't fight, we'll be the negotiators
'Cause we try to save our skin from being hurt

We are so superficial when for stars we are only dirt
That is a painful culmination we must face dead in the eyes
As stars are fed up with all our cries.

Suicide

Oh, if I have told you how many times
I wanted to give up after countless tries
It would be so simple to just stop everything
But the truth is, it's your family.
Who deals with all the sorrow bearing?
I may be free, but everyone else is in agony.
So, I live my life until it stops
Until it finally hits its last clocks.

I teared up too much and not smiled enough
And it was not that even life was tough
Seemed more like I was born
With this sadness, like an endless torn
I was made just to wander without purpose
Going there and here, without fear to lose
No insane gamble against my faith
And no compromises in its challenges trade.
I may lack a direction in this existence
But maybe my time will come with some
resistance.

Searching

How many beds and hearts
Do I still need to encounter?
Before I can finish my thirsts
For your skin over mine, in full surrender.
How many failed dates
That my heart hates
Do I need to have with no gain?
Before I can end this pain.
Your eyes still haunt me
And won't let me be.
No matter how hard I try
I see them everywhere and I cry.
I cry my soul out after our memories
I am a fool who looks for fairies
In a world that is only grey
For an old and dusty month of May.
I can still feel your touch
It burns me like a torch
Although time passed mercilessly
And in your memories, I'm faceless.
I can't stop wishing for our rencounter
The beats of my heart are its counter
As if that meeting won't prevail
I should go in death with a hail.

Time on Earth

I painted flowers on my skin
So, I could be a garden too keen
For any stranger to ignore
My eyes are stars that lure
Men and women to their damnation
And I don't use any incantation.
Though my words are enchanted
And my attention was hardly granted.
My voice can be sweet as a lullaby
Or harsh that I make you cry, baby.
So, mind your steps in front of me
Watch your words and seek the key
To my eternal devotion for you
And may you find magic in life too.
But don't be too afraid of eternity
As Eden may be a garden of felicity
If you only dare to live a life with correctness
Even when you may lack life sweet directness.

Art in pain

I can smell the start of summer
As the wind sings like a hummer
I can feel the heat in my body
But my heart can feel it hardly.
It's been cold for countless days
Since one day it has parted with all ties
Without thinking about consequences
Or the loneliness expenses.
On an isolated island full of remorse
From all the past ghosts that walk
Around it, acting like a disdain lock
For, the heart that threw them away with force.
It's a lonely heart in a body still cursed
By the lost connections and that's not the worst
As nobody tries to approach anymore
The heart that acted like a whore.
So, here I am waiting for freedom
So that my soul enters a happy kingdom
Where it won't be afraid
That once again it'll be led
By the same treacherous heart
That made the soul believe that art
Could be found only on a lonely path
That it comes only from wrath.

Her voice

Her hair was long and tangled
And her voice was always strangled
By strong emotions that visited her veins.
She always wondered which reins
Is it the heart or the mind?
Or none of the kind?
Who chose when to speak up?
And when to shut up...
Her conscience belittled her capacity
Of surviving her anxiety fantasy
It was only the smallest spark of hope
That made her spirit try and cope
With her existence toughest moments.
Marvellous to see its true endowments
Standing out to fight an invisible enemy
Like winning is the only option in her destiny.
Oh, but her eyes were another story
The spark in her sight is damnatory
It condemns any soul against her will
It turns all into stone and keeps still.
There's no mercy left in their depths
It is just despair and the look of the deaths
That her heart witnessed some ancient night
When there was no knight in sight
To save her heart, from soaking

She knows that's only foolish thinking.
As nobody could've saved her that time
It is only a wishful desire to escape a crime
She inflicted through herself by choice
That's how she lost the power of her voice.

Lesson

I've learnt that no friend no matter how old
Is worth shutting your voice, having your heart go cold
I've learnt there is no boy that is worth tears
Better use that time to evolve and kill your fears
I've learnt that no job will keep you happy
If all you get from it is money, it'll feel crappy
I've learnt that at the end of the day you are alone
Impregnate a healthy cope mechanism down to the core
I've learnt that before you try to save someone
You better take care of yourself, or you'll burn down.
I've learnt that is good to have a plan
But you should be flexible as much as you can
I've learnt that fame comes hand in hand with despair
There's no way you'll escape critics even if you take care
Of your image, even privacy it comes in shortage
So, no amount of fame could be dealt without rage.
I've learnt that when all seems cluttered

You should just take a pen and write
Until reality doesn't feel so altered
And your thoughts feel finally right.

Loneliness

Sunkissed in my dreams
Rained in my reality realms
I would keep my eyes shut
Maybe there won't be any shout
From other people to tell me
How to live my life, who to be
I would rather rethink my existence
Then attempt any kind of resistance
Against norms and rules of society
But would that only enfold me in falsity?
I wasn't born to be afraid
I wasn't born to yield
I may have been born while I cried
But I was taught how to hide
Nobody taught me how to ride
Depression and oppression
It was deemed out of fashion.
If only I had more people to protect me
Maybe life wouldn't have got me on my knee
So often as it managed to
But I emerged out of my sorrows too
With nobody around to clap
But with some to get me into a trap
Out of jealousy and incapability
From their part - stupidness remains a fatality.

A moment in infinity

Let my fingers stroke your hair
So that your hairsprings can feel my care
As it propagates through your whole existence
And you are assured by my consistence.
Let my cheek on your chest
Let my soul get some rest
As your breath always calmed storms
And I feel the safest in your arms.
Let me hear the vibrations of your voice
Indulge me in this silly choice
As you may never know
When this tranquillity will blow
And all it could be lost
In a matter of seconds that cost
Our happiness that should have been indulged
In an infinity lake without all that disturbing
bulge.
So, before I worry about unfounded concerns
Let's have some tenderness turns
As our love is too sweet to be postponed
And I may want to let life be stoned.

Healing

How can I fly with broken wings
How should I escape from the fire rings
Will I be able to emerge from this trash
Or I am only meant to turn into ash?
I am surrounded by lost thoughts
I am afraid in hell, I may cross
If I don't pay attention to my courage
As it has with fear a toxic marriage.
I can't get drowned in the venom of love
As from that battle no peace dove
Could be used to save my heart
And my brain in love is not that smart.
My broken wings get rained on
By my sorrowful tears until dawn.
When the light finally emerges, it cleans
My scars up to the point it enters my genes.
It washes away the sorrows from my whole
body
To the point, I can't remember being hurt by
somebody.
My soul remembers how to thank the universe
How to take care of others scars and nurse
Lost souls that seek the same healing.
It is no secret recipe of love revealing
Only the power of forgiving your mistakes
That's the wild card to play at all stakes.

All in vain

I remember the first time when I heard
"We can't be friends" and my world fell apart
I was expecting to lose him after breaking his heart
But I still hoped that it wouldn't happen to us this part.

What could I've said after all?
"Don't leave me as a friend just stall
You promised long ago at the start
That no matter what
You will stay and be a part
Of my life 'till death do us apart."

Silly girl, believing an in-love student boy
He eventually forgot his promise – he was coy.
I knew I deserve his disappearance
But I needed in my heart some clearance.
Two years of purgatory were enough
I couldn't stay to be another day tough
I was thirsty after my forgotten freedom
Hence, I burned down our relationship kingdom.
So now, I am lonely, with no desire to love again
For me, love was and is all in vain.

I don't want to get married anymore
I only want my feelings shut down to the core.

Can you let me be "happily ever after" by myself?
Can you let me be the book without a reader on an empty shelf?
I am sorry, I can't see the beauty of falling in love
In the end… they all leave – there is no true love
It's just false hope and pure insanity
A contest with endless prejudice and vanity.
Finally, it's just a person you decide to stop to
Because you're too tired of searching another Waterloo.
But life goes on, so deep down my soul still hopes
That my brain is not right, it's just the way it copes
With this cruel endless life
That one day I will be a wife.

www.ingramcontent.com/pod-product-compliance
Lightning Source LLC
Chambersburg PA
CBHW051752130826
49812CB00033B/1108